WEEKLY WR READER®
EARLY LEARNING LIBRARY

Animals That Live in the Mountains/ Animales de las montañas

Condors/Cóndor

by/por JoAnn Early Macken

Reading consultant/Consultora de lectura:
Susan Nations, M.Ed.,
author/literacy coach/consultant in literacy development
autora/tutora de alfabetización/
consultora de desarrollo de la lectura

Please visit our web site at: www.earlyliteracy.cc
For a free color catalog describing **Weekly Reader**® Early Learning Library's list
of high-quality books, call 1-877-445-5824 (USA) or 1-800-387-3178 (Canada).
Weekly Reader® Early Learning Library's fax: (414) 336-0164.

Library of Congress Cataloging-in-Publication Data

Macken, JoAnn Early, 1953-
    [Condors. Spanish & English]
    Condors = Cóndor / by JoAnn Early Macken.
        p. cm. — (Animals that live in the mountains = Animales de las montañas)
    Includes bibliographical references and index.
    ISBN 0-8368-6447-6 (lib. bdg.)
    ISBN 0-8368-6454-9 (softcover)
    1. Condors—Juvenile literature.   I. Title: Cóndor.   II. Title.
    QL696.C53M32   2006
    598.9'2—dc22
                                                                    2005033289

This edition first published in 2006 by
Weekly Reader® **Early Learning Library**
A Member of the WRC Media Family of Companies
330 West Olive Street, Suite 100
Milwaukee, WI 53212 USA

Managing editor: Valerie J. Weber
Art direction: Tammy West
Cover design and page layout: Kami Strunsee
Picture research: Diane Laska-Swanke
Translators: Tatiana Acosta and Guillermo Gutiérrez

Picture credits: Cover, © Randy Collyer/Visuals Unlimited; pp. 5, 7, 15, 17, 21 U.S. Fish and Wildlife Service;
p. 9 © Tom Vezo/naturepl.com; pp. 11, 19 © Daniel Gomez/naturepl.com; p. 13 © Gabriel Rojo/naturepl.com.

Printed in the United States of America

1 2 3 4 5 6 7 8 9 10 09 08 07 06

Note to Educators and Parents

Reading is such an exciting adventure for young children! They are beginning to integrate their oral language skills with written language. To encourage children along the path to early literacy, books must be colorful, engaging, and interesting; they should invite the young reader to explore both the print and the pictures.

Animals That Live in the Mountains is a new series designed to help children read about creatures that make their homes in high places. Each book describes a different mountain animal's life cycle, behavior, and habitat.

Each book is specially designed to support the young reader in the reading process. The familiar topics are appealing to young children and invite them to read — and reread — again and again. The full-color photographs and enhanced text further support the student during the reading process.

In addition to serving as wonderful picture books in schools, libraries, homes, and other places where children learn to love reading, these books are specifically intended to be read within an instructional guided reading group. This small group setting allows beginning readers to work with a fluent adult model as they make meaning from the text. After children develop fluency with the text and content, the book can be read independently. Children and adults alike will find these books supportive, engaging, and fun!

— Susan Nations, M.Ed., author, literacy coach,
and consultant in literacy development

Nota para los maestros y los padres

¡Leer es una aventura tan emocionante para los niños pequeños! A esta edad están comenzando a integrar su manejo del lenguaje oral con el lenguaje escrito. Para animar a los niños en el camino de la lectura incipiente, los libros deben ser coloridos, estimulantes e interesantes; deben invitar a los jóvenes lectores a explorar la letra impresa y las ilustraciones.

Animales de las montañas es una nueva colección diseñada para presentar a los jóvenes lectores algunos animales que viven en regiones montañosas. Cada libro explica, en un lenguaje sencillo y fácil de leer, el ciclo de vida, el comportamiento y el hábitat de un animal de las montañas.

Cada libro está especialmente diseñado para ayudar a los jóvenes lectores en el proceso de lectura. Los temas familiares llaman la atención de los niños y los invitan a leer — y releer — una y otra vez. Las fotografías a todo color y el tamaño de la letra ayudan aún más al estudiante en el proceso de lectura.

Además de servir como maravillosos libros ilustrados en escuelas, bibliotecas, hogares y otros lugares donde los niños aprenden a amar la lectura, estos libros han sido especialmente concebidos para ser leídos en un grupo de lectura guiada. Este contexto permite que los lectores incipientes trabajen con un adulto que domina la lectura mientras van determinando el significado del texto. Una vez que los niños dominan el texto y el contenido, el libro puede ser leído de manera independiente. ¡Estos libros les resultarán útiles, estimulantes y divertidos a niños y a adultos por igual!

— Susan Nations, M.Ed., autora/tutora de alfabetización/
consultora de desarrollo de la lectura

Condors have shiny black feathers. Parts of their wings are white. White or black feathers circle their necks. Few feathers grow on their heads.

Los cóndores tienen un plumaje negro brillante. Partes de sus alas son blancas. Alrededor del cuello tienen plumas blancas o negras. En la cabeza apenas les crecen plumas.

Condors are huge! They are the largest flying land birds. Their wings are wide. Their legs are long. Their long toes have claws, or **talons**.

━━━━━━━━━━━━━━━━━━

¡Los cóndores son enormes! Son las aves terrestres voladoras más grandes. Sus alas son muy anchas. Sus patas son largas. Sus largos dedos tienen **garras**.

talons/
garras

7

Condors glide on the wind like kites. They soar on warm air currents. They do not often flap their wings.

Los cóndores planean en el aire como papalotes. Se elevan con las corrientes de aire caliente. Apenas baten las alas.

9

Condors live and eat in groups. They follow each other to food. They see and hear well, but they cannot smell well.

- - - - - - - - - - - - - - - - - -

Los cóndores viven y se alimentan en grupos. Para encontrar comida siguen a los demás. Pueden ver y oír bien, pero su olfato no es bueno.

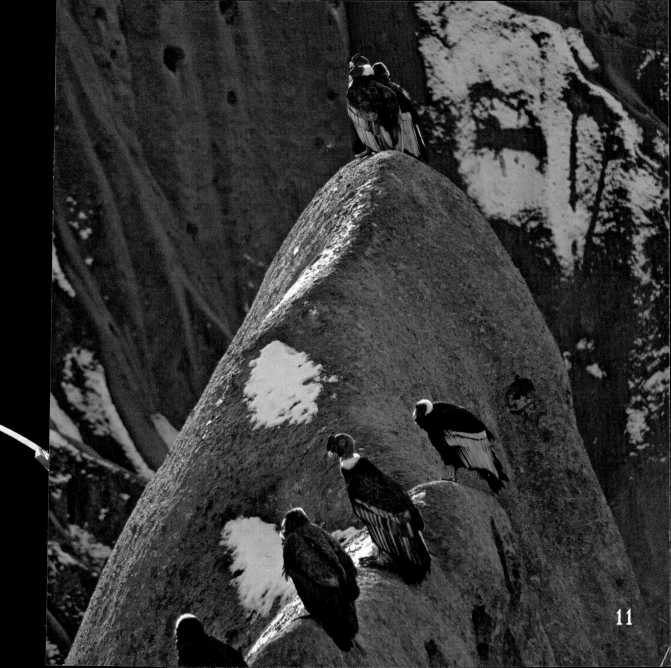

11

Condors do not kill other animals. They mainly eat dead animals. With their strong beaks, they tear meat apart.

Los cóndores no matan a otros animales. Sobre todo, se alimentan de animales muertos. Desgarran la carne con sus fuertes picos.

beaks/
picos

13

Not many condors are left in the world.
Many were shot. Some died from
poison. Now people are working to
keep condors safe.

No quedan muchos cóndores en el
mundo. A muchos les dispararon.
Otros murieron envenenados. Ahora
se está trabajando para proteger a
los cóndores.

A baby condor is called a **chick**. A person feeds this chick with a puppet. The puppet looks like a condor.

━ ━ ━ ━ ━ ━ ━ ━ ━ ━ ━ ━ ━ ━ ━

Una cría de cóndor es un **polluelo**. Una persona alimenta a este polluelo con un muñeco. El muñeco parece un cóndor.

puppet/
muñeco

17

At three months old, a chick flaps its wings. It grows new dark feathers. By six months old, it begins to fly.

A los tres meses, un polluelo puede batir las alas. Le crecen plumas nuevas, de color negro. A los seis meses de edad, el polluelo comienza a volar.

People raised these condors and then set them free. Now condors fly over the mountains again.

Estos cóndores fueron criados por personas y después liberados. Ahora, los cóndores vuelven a volar sobre las montañas.

Glossary

currents — flowing air or water

flap — move back and forth or up and down

follow — to go after

glides — moves smoothly

poison — something that causes illness or death when eaten or drunk

Glosario

batir — mover las alas

corrientes — masas de aire o de agua en movimiento

planear — volar sin mover las alas

seguir — ir detrás

veneno — algo que produce malestar o la muerte cuando se come o se bebe

For More Information/Más información

Books

California Condor. Welcome Books (series).
   Edana Eckart (Children's Press)

California Condors. Patricia A. Fink Martin
   (Children's Press)

Libros

Aves (Birds). Ted O'Hare (Rourke)

Los pájaros/Birds.   Jennifer Blizin Gillis (Heinemann)

Web Sites/Páginas web
California Condor
El cóndor de California
www.npca.org/wildlife_protection/wildlife_facts/condor.asp
Pictures and facts about condors in national parks
Fotografías e información de los cóndores en los
parques nacionales

Index

Índice

About the Author

JoAnn Early Macken is the author of two rhyming picture books, *Sing-Along Song* and *Cats on Judy*, and more than eighty nonfiction books for children. Her poems have appeared in several children's magazines. A graduate of the M.F.A. in Writing for Children and Young Adults Program at Vermont College, she lives in Wisconsin with her husband and their two sons.

Información sobre la autora

JoAnn Early Macken ha escrito dos libros de rimas con ilustraciones, *Sing-Along Song* y *Cats on Judy*, y más de ochenta libros de no ficción para niños. Sus poemas han sido publicados en varias revistas infantiles. JoAnn se graduó en el programa M.F.A de Escritura para Niños y Jóvenes de Vermont College. Vive en Wisconsin con su esposo y sus dos hijos.